better together*

*This book is best read together, grownup and kid.

 akidsco.com

a
kids
book
about

a kids book about

PUBLIC))) SPEAKING

by **TED**ˣPortland

a
kids
book
about

Printed in the United States of America.

A Kids Book About books are available online: *akidsco.com*

To share your stories, ask questions, or inquire about bulk
purchases (schools, libraries, and nonprofits), please use
the following email address: *hello@akidsco.com*

ISBN: 978-1-953955-66-1

Designed by Gabby Nguyen
Edited by Jennifer Goldstein

This book is dedicated to every thinker, doer, and creator. Don't be afraid to use your voice for good.

Speak up!

Intro

ommunication through public speaking is a learned skill that can open possibilities and growth in all of us.

We wanted to write this book to illustrate the basic skills associated with public speaking and the profound benefits it offers—developing leadership skills, enriching confidence, influencing the world around you, and becoming a go-to person for ideas and solutions.

Whether in your community, your school, at the dinner table, or on your sports team, public speaking is a way to bring people together. And most importantly, with confidence in their public speaking skills, kids can feel empowered to call out issues they see and voice their opinion on how to improve them!

As you read this book with your future changemaker, emphasize that public speaking is all about sharing your knowledge about a topic with others in a compelling way which motivates everyone to move toward good and positive change.

This is a book about PUBLIC SPEAKING.

In its simplest form, public speaking is **sharing your ideas out loud to an audience.**

We believe everyone has something important to say.

Yes, even you!

And we hope this book will help you find a way to share your ideas with others.

Let's be honest,
public speaking can be
kind of **scary.**

So many things could happen
while you're up there
in front of everyone.

You could get nervous.

Or forget what you're
going to say.

And what if people judge you?

That all sounds awful.

But what if we told you public speaking could be kind of amazing?

That it could make you feel really proud and strong?

And hey, it might even be fun too!

We also believe more than anything else that public speaking **can help others.**

So, who are we?

Cathey, Greg, Stephen, Jelani, David, and Amy.

We are public speakers and coaches who help others **(like you)** get up in front of people to share something important.

In this book, each of us will pop in with thoughts and ideas.

We'll put them on little sticky notes so you'll know it's one of us.

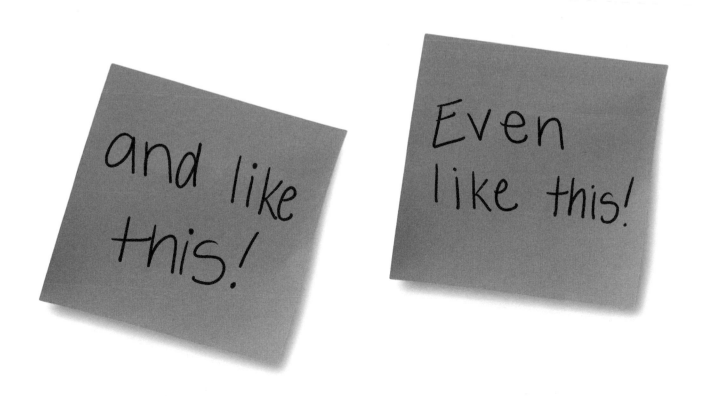

So what is public speaking really?

Public speaking is putting yourself out in front of an audience* to share your ideas, stories, and the things you know with the people there.

*Audience just means a group of people.

Public speaking can happen in your **class, community, home, or up on stage.**

One time I spoke at a baseball stadium.

- Jelani

For example:

Imagine that 1 week from today, your assignment is to talk to your whole class about the solar system.

You'll be the only one talking, and what you share needs to last at least 5 minutes.

How does that make you feel?

It might make you wake up in the middle of the night with your heart racing.

It might give you butterflies or make you feel sick to your stomach.

It might make you worry you'll forget what you're supposed to say.

What you're feeling when any of those things happen is fear.

Fear that you might mess up or that everyone will laugh at you.

But we want you
to know something.

Something **so important** we want
to make sure you really hear us...

Ever feels

yone fear.

Feeling fear is totally **normal.**

And did you know that our bodies feel **anxious** and **excited** in the same kind of way?

Like, our bodies can't tell the difference between the two.

For instance, your heart might beat fast and your palms might get really sweaty when people clap for you at the end of a performance—which is a really exciting thing!

But your palms might get sweaty and your heart might beat fast when you are afraid something bad will happen too.

Your body is reacting in exactly the same way to 2 entirely different emotions. So even though you may feel nervous about public speaking, **it can also be exciting!**

Remember what we said about helping others? Well, sharing your ideas can inspire others.

Your ideas could help someone learn something new.

Your personal story could help someone else feel less alone.

Your words could lead to important change!

It can be a gift to someone.
- Greg

Because guess what?!

You have
impo

rtant

things to say!

Would you like to know
our best piece of advice
for public speaking?

Here it goes...

Just be you!

Don't try to be like everyone else.

Some kids like sports.

Some kids like music.

Some kids like juggling.

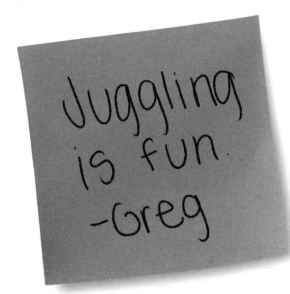

Some kids like being in rodeos.

Our differences
make us **interesting.**

You gotta just be you!

It's way better when
we aren't all the same.

And that's true
when we speak too.

**We should feel like ourselves,
and talk like ourselves.**

And here's a little secret.

Don't worry about being perfect.

Because guess what—

you can't be!

All speakers make mistakes, even teachers and grownups.

Really great speakers learn to laugh at their mistakes instead of feeling bad about them.

When mistakes happen, shrug it off and keep going.
– Amy

So don't try to be perfect.

Practice is really what will make you feel more comfortable.

And the more you do something, the less scary it becomes.

Making your practice **playful** helps a lot too.

Maybe that looks like standing in your kitchen telling your grownup about Saturn's rings.

Or sitting on your bed talking to a poster about the stars in the solar system.

especially if it's an awesome poster!
-Jelani

When you practice, you'll learn how you communicate.

Practicing might help you notice that you

talk fast,

sway back and forth,

tap your foot,

or want to read all your words from a notecard.

These are all good things
to recognize so you can
work on them.

Like if you talk fast,
your friends might not hear all
the great stuff you want to share!

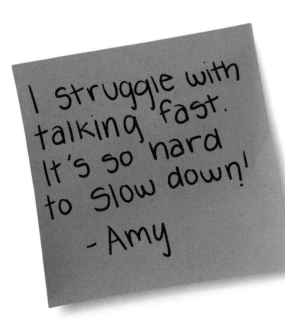

I struggle with
talking fast.
It's so hard
to slow down!
   - Amy

Or if you sway, they may get distracted watching you instead of listening to you!

If you read all your words from a notecard, they may feel like you're talking at them, not with them.

Practice makes permanent.
-Cathey

When we speak, we want people

to listen ideas an

to our
d stories.

Why?

Because our ideas can be interesting and helpful!

They can even change the world!

So, how can you become a better speaker so people will want to listen?

We have 3 ideas for you.

One. Talk to 1 person at a time.

Talk to them like you're talking with a friend.

Look them in the eye so they feel connected to you when you speak.

Eye contact is one of the best ways to look confident in front of a group of people!

-Amy

Two. **Speak clearly.**

That might mean speaking more slowly or loudly.

Remember, people want to hear your ideas!

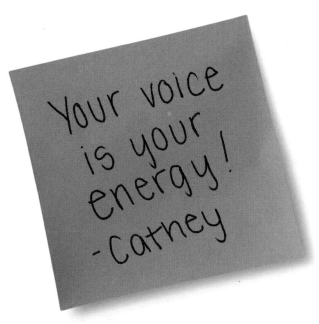

Your voice is your energy!
-Cathey

Three. Talk with passion.

Don't be afraid to gesture with your hands.

Sound excited in your voice.

Believe in what you're saying.

If you look and sound like you care about your ideas, your listeners will care too!

You've got this!

It may feel awkward
or even scary, **but be yourself!**

Practice your ideas
out loud,
 **a lot.**

Connect with the
people listening to you.

And remember...

You have someth say and your

ing important to
ideas matter.

Outro

Now that we have begun to face our fears and develop fundamental public speaking skills, our hope is to help kids continue to grow in their ability to effectively communicate and drive positive change.

Whether the goal is to engage in thoughtful debate, make a career as a motivational speaker, or gain confidence in front of an audience, public speaking can help kids achieve their dreams. This book is just the first step in that journey.

One of the often unexpected delights of public speaking is how it builds confidence. Encourage your kid to speak boldly and often about what they're passionate about, and guide them in using that passion to spark change. Let's work together to unlock our kids' potential through the power of communicating with our words!

About TED^xPortland

TEDxPortland produces experiences to create space for people to come together to spark deep discussion and connection. Established in 1984, TED stands for Technology, Entertainment, Design, and "TED Talks" explore these 3 subject areas that collectively shape our world. In 2009, TEDx was established, with x referring to an independently organized TED event. Portland was an early adopter with a license to organize a local event showcasing ordinary speakers with extraordinary ideas.

About Our Contributors

Greg Bell (he/him)
Watch his **TED** Talk
Water the Bamboo
From April 30, 2011

Cathey Armillas (she/her)
Speaker/Story Coach!
Watch her **TED** Talk
Share Your Life
From May 10, 2014

Stephen Green (he/him)
Watch his **TED** Talk
Cheat More
From April 15, 2017

David Rae (he/him)
Curator **TED**^xPortland

Amy Wolff (she/her)
Speaker Coach!
Watch her **TED** Talk
Discovering Hope As Your Agency
From May 28, 2022

Jelani Memory (he/him)
Watch his **TED** Talk
Kids Are Ready
From May 28, 2022

find more kids books about

And share your own story!

incarceration, self-love, identity, cancer, confidence, trauma, life online, adventure, war, body image, and anxiety.

a akidsco.com